LIVING WITH
FETAL ALCOHOL SYNDROME:
OUR JOURNEY WITH TISHA

Compiled by Peter and Vivien Lourens - FASIC South Africa
In collaboration with Sophia Warner and Sandra Marais

Fetal Alcohol Spectrum Disorder (FASD) is the name given to a spectrum of birth defects produced in an infant whose mother drank alcohol during her pregnancy. Fetal Alcohol Syndrome (FAS) is the most severe category in the spectrum.

September 9, 2012

BACKGROUND TO THE HANDBOOK AND ABOUT THE LOURENS FAMILY

Peter, Andrew, Vivien, David and Bridget
Carrie, Mindy, Tisha, Claire, Olivia and Leigh-Anne

These are our children:......... with Tisha aged 8 in the fore-front

Peter and I are foster parents to a young lady who we have had since just after she was born in 1996. She has Fetal Alcohol Syndrome. We were emergency foster parents with Cape Town Child Welfare for sixteen years and in that time had many babies with Fetal Alcohol Syndrome. My eldest son lives with his wife and three daughters in America. We have three children living at home as our second son now has a house of his own. I have a background of child care, particularly special needs children.

In 1999, we started the first International Fetal Alcohol Syndrome Day in South Africa and each year on the 9th day of the 9th month at 9h09 we have been involved in creating awareness on this day.

I was persuaded to write this handbook as it was found that there was little practical help for handling children with FAS. This was also what motivated us to start FASIC, as when I needed help I couldn't find any in South Africa.

We were emergency foster parents for Child Welfare from 1989 – 2006 and were used to dealing with many different problems when asked to take a baby. So it wasn't unusual to get a call asking to take a premature baby with only an hour's notice.

So it was in 1996 with Tisha, little did we know the journey we would take with her. When I was handed the tiny shaking premature baby, I was told she was a "fail to thrive" baby who probably would not last the weekend

Tisha at 10 weeks old

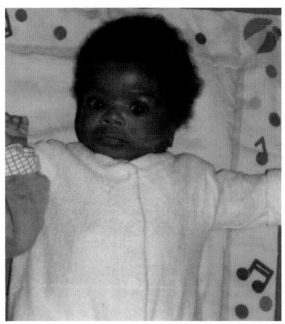

Since 1996, we have run the Fetal Alcohol Syndrome Information Centre (FASIC) from our home, situated in Pinelands, Cape Town

Our logo is the FAS knot, around the word FASIC.

- The knot is made of white cord and is tied in a reef knot. The knot symbolizes many things.

- The circle symbolises the womb, the baby's head, the human brain and the world.

- The cord that joins us all together in caring

- The reef knot cannot be broken or snapped, the more you pull the tighter the bond.

- The frayed ends represent the damaged nervous system which cannot be repaired.

The knot was designed by Brian Philcox of Canada who is a father of an adopted daughter with FAS.

FASIC can provide

- Presentations

- FAS leaflets

- Information by phone or e mail

- DVDs

- Support

- Referrals

- FAS Manual: this manual offers practical help for care givers of babies and children with FAS and is based on our knowledge and experience. We belong to a world-wide link and the people on this list have been an incredible help to us and are a huge source of information.

This hand book is based on our personal experiences and from the knowledge we have gained as foster parents to a large number of babies who were in our care. It is not based on any medical or scientific research findings.

For more information please contact us:

fasinfocentre@mweb.co.za

0825099530

GLOSSARY OF TERMS:

FETAL ALCOHOL SPECTRUM DISORDER (FASD) describes the range of effects that can occur when an individual is prenatally exposed to alcohol.

FASD includes:

- Fetal Alcohol Syndrome (FAS) is the most severe category followed by -

- Partial Fetal Alcohol Syndrome (PFAS)

- Alcohol-Related Neuro-developmental Disorders (ARND)

- Alcohol-Related Birth Defects (ARBD)

FAS(D) may also lead to severe social and psychological consequences for the individual child and for the family because of the child's mental and behavioural handicap.

INDEX TO TOPICS
COVERED IN THIS HANDBOOK

CHAPTER 1
MEDICAL ISSUES

The Center for Disease Control in the USA defines Fetal Alcohol Syndrome as the severe end of a spectrum of harmful effects caused by maternal alcohol use during pregnancy. It is also one of the leading causes of preventable birth defects and developmental disabilities globally.

There is no cure,
it is 100% preventable and
100% irreversible.

The signs and symptoms of FAS manifests mainly in three primary symptom categories:

1. Growth deficiency starting prenatally – low birth weight, small head circumference, failure to thrive.

2. Central nervous system (CNS) dysfunction – microcephaly (small head and brain), delayed development, behavioural problems such as hyperactivity, inability to concentrate, impulsiveness, attention deficit, ie difficulty recalling and remembering information, learning disabilities, poor memory, inability to understand concepts such as time, poor problem-solving skills, poor coordination/fine motor skills, epilepsy. Because of the nature of damage to the CNS, abnormalities of organs and limbs can also occur, such as cardiac, ocular, auditory and renal problems.

3. A specific pattern of facial characteristics including smaller eye openings, flattened check bones, thin and smooth upper lip (see sketch).

There is a need for at least yearly physical examinations of the child.

FAS children tend to be very fragile.

Their early months are particularly plagued with illness and stress as their systems flush the alcohol from their bodies.

They often require the care of doctors and specialists who will prescribe medicines and treatments.

A FAS baby or infant is likely to exhibit behaviour such as:

- Irritability

- Crying a lot

- Sleep disturbances

- Feeding problems

FAS children DO NOT 'grow out of it' – the growth retardation is likely to continue throughout life.

Fetal Alcohol Syndrome is a birth defect caused by the mother drinking alcohol whilst pregnant. No amount of alcohol has been proved to be safe, so it is wise to say that no alcohol should be consumed during pregnancy.

Pre-natal exposure to alcohol can cause an array of effects. These largely depend on when and how much alcohol is consumed. It is not only the alcoholic mother but any mother who drinks alcohol when pregnant who is putting her baby at risk of having multiple problems.

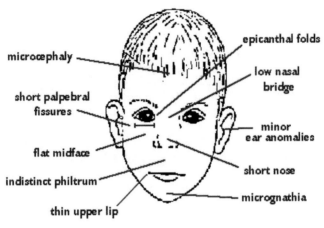

A characteristic face.

- ☐ Short Palpebral fissures (eye slits)

- ☐ A short upturned nose

- ☐ A smooth or long philtrum (the ridge between nose and lips)

- ☐ Thin upper lip

- ☐ A flat mid face

Growth deficiency—either pre or post natal for height, weight or both.

Central nervous system damage

Microcephaly (small brain)

Tremors

Fine or gross motor problems or both

Behavioural problems

Developmental delays

Mental delays

Organ damage

A pre natal history is vital as FAS can only be diagnosed by a specialist.

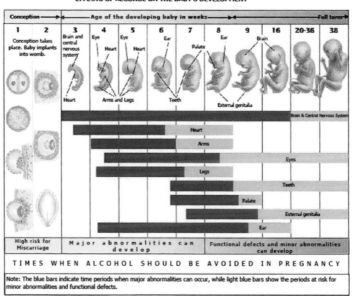

EFFECTS OF ALCOHOL ON THE BABY'S DEVELOPMENT

The chart above shows the developmental stages of the fetus indicating the development of specific organs and limbs at specific stages of growth. The blue lines indicate when, in the development of the fetus, the greatest damage can be done by exposure to alcohol. It is clearly indicated that most damage is done in the early stages of pregnancy and that damage to the central nervous system can continue throughout the pregnancy.

Below is a picture of a normal brain with next to it a picture of an alcohol damaged brain.

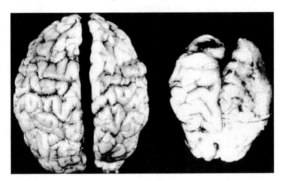

The following are the clinic cards of my two daughters Leigh-Anne and Tisha (a child with FAS).

The girls had the same milk formula and baby foods. It can clearly be seen how each of them progressed. Tisha hardly put on any weight and each gram was an achievement. I also wrote on the bottom of Tisha's chart her milestones. It is clear that Tisha's development lagged far behind her sister's but due to intensive physiotherapy were a lot better than expected.

Tisha

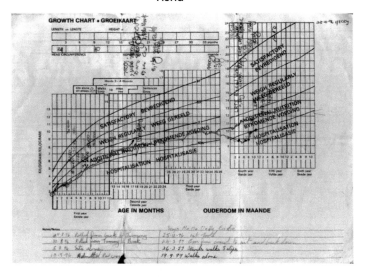

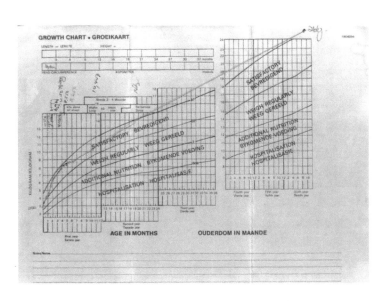

Enjoying a day at the beach –
Tisha at one year old

CHAPTER 2
BEHAVIOUR ISSUES AND MANAGEMENT IN LEARNING ENVIRONMENTS

Tisha used to have severe temper tantrums and throw herself backwards. This was due to frustration as she could not express herself in words. This lessened as she learned to talk. Now if something frustrates her, she runs from the room but cannot tell what causes it.

The behaviours exhibited in children with FASD require not just adequate learning environments, but optimal ones. Tendencies for distractibility, hyperactivity and other disruptions such as aggressiveness compete with the child's desire to learn and interfere with his or her effectiveness in completing the task at hand. The teacher/caregivers may be kept busy managing challenging behaviour rather than teaching.

Lectures about appropriate behaviour have no meaning for students with FASD. Choice making is a difficult skill for alcohol-affected children to learn and is often circumvented by impulsiveness.

Identify behaviours, not characteristics. Poor memory is a characteristic of FASD. Management of specific tasks requiring memory, such as remaining focused, can be remedied with appropriate strategies.

Teachers, caregivers and others need to assess their own support system and themselves. They need to have a clear understanding of behavioural goals. They need to set clear goals for themselves and the child. All who work with FASD children should identify and consistently apply behaviour management techniques that are effective with the individual child.

Quickly deal with inappropriate behaviour. Time out, when the child has had the technique explained, is effective with younger children. Social deprivation is also effective because of the touchy-feely nature of FASD children. Behaviour contracts and frequent reminders of class rules are also effective.

Timing is when a set time is given for doing a task or for "time out" for bad behaviour. The latter must be short as if too long the child will become bored which could lead to more bad behaviour. Praise for sitting still.

Timing can head off many problems and rewards the child for appropriate behaviour without interrupting him/her. This technique can be used to strengthen individual play and independent working skills. It may be also useful to structure a daily report card so that the parent, guardian or some other caring adult will know about the child's successes and can reinforce appropriate behaviour.

Psychiatric therapy can also be indicated. Psychiatry is not as useful to these children as behaviourist teaching therapies. The children enjoy the interest of an adult and can become dependent upon the attention they receive. Meanwhile, the problems do not get solved because they are birth defect based, not psyche based. Psychiatrists and school psychologists need to approach the child from a behavioural viewpoint, targeting specific actions, such as impulsivity. Use concrete hands-on techniques to help the child.

Alcohol affected children tend to be extreme in their feelings. Rage is a particularly difficult expression for the teacher/caregiver to handle. In doing so, they need to first determine the cause. Rage can be related to an inability to communicate, exhaustion or hunger, wilfulness, failure to adequately transition or an expression of memory deficit frustration.

Help meet the child's need by exploring the cause of the rage. Model alternative ways to express the need. Anticipate and work to prevent rages by providing snacks, using time out providing thorough explanations, and teaching students how to deal with anger on a one on one basis.

Teach patience as part of the curriculum.
"I want, won't get.
Please may I, sometimes does."
is a simple rule that
helps control impulsiveness.

Planning also needs to be directly taught. Make schedules for class work, play, and activities. List work tasks in order of doing them. Use art for smaller children, dovetailing it with language concepts and vocabulary.

The outside community has large expectations. The hidden nature of FASD encourages misunderstandings. Few people understand that the cause of the child's poor social behaviour is a damaged brain. FASD children should be taught life skills so that they can be prepared to live in the community. Provide "Rules to Live By" which are simple and concise. When going on outings, repeat the relevant rule every single time. Make sure rules are clearly understood and enforce consistently.

Independence is necessary for the well-being of the child. Practice it in small steps that can be managed.

Remember:
Teach, model, train, self-management.

Advocacy is a prime need for FASD students. They need someone to watch over them and to help them in cognitive, behavioural and social situations. Caregivers or other family members can be the best advocate because they have contact with all facets of the child's life. But it is easy for caregivers to believe they don't have the knowledge or skills to do what is best for the child. There would also be instances where an outsider can see more clearly what is required for the child.

To summarize:

- Change expectations but don't lower them.

- Make plans with the reality of FASD in mind.

- Plan with the end in mind.

- See FASD children as they can be when the challenges they bring with them are met.

- View them proactively.

- Look at them as having the potential to be Olympic athletes and university scholars.

- Stay creative in the approaches used.

- If we believe we can, we will.

- Visualize ways to overcome, or circumvent problems.

- See these learners as fully grown adults, responsible for themselves. From there, determine what it will take to achieve that end.

- Look at the needs for education, for experience, for resources and then pursue those things that will meet the challenges of homes, classrooms, and communities changed by FASD children.

MANAGING HYPER-ACTIVITY

> We have found that hyperactivity can be controlled with management skills. Once when Tisha was a little excited in a shop, while she and Peter were waiting at the check-out, she announced to every one that she was a bit hyper!

- Organised exercises before settling down to school work is a very good idea. This does not mean play time where they are running around unsupervised.

- Catching the problem before it starts will avoid confrontation so the signs must be recognised.

- A cardboard frame around the child will help concentration.

Below is a list of ways to help manage hyperactivity

- Keep the environment structured.

- Make a picture calendar. For instance, make a board with hooks and laminate pictures of activities for the whole day. Have another picture of child taking jacket off and hanging up the jacket. Have a picture of a child putting puzzle together.

- As the child completes each activity during the day, the child would take the picture off the hook, turn it over, and hang the picture back on the hook. The child knows that he/she has completed the activity.

- Give the child a choice from 2 or 3 toys. Give the child plenty of time to make a choice. If the child seems to be having difficulty making a choice, watch the child to see if he/she looks longer at a particular toy or makes a movement toward a certain toy.

- Have a "start" and "finish" box for each activity.

- Keep the designated activities in the same place. The child will know where to return the activity when he/she is finished.

- Sit on a chair rather than on the floor. The chair keeps the child from leaning backward, forward and sideways. The chair helps keep the child in a specific space.

- The teacher may need to show the child how to sit on the chair.

- Feet flat on the floor this is very important as it makes the child feel 'grounded'. If the child's feet do not touch the floor books or a block of wood should be used.

- Then hands on the side, sitting up straight.

- Have the activity at the table ready for the child when the child is sitting properly

- Minimize waiting time

- Structure the day alternating quiet time, active time, quiet time, active time, etc. Have as few rules as possible and enforce rules consistently.

- Never make a rule you do not plan to enforce.

- Avoid threats.

- Take photos of child doing activities that occur during the day as children love to see themselves and it keeps a record of behaviour. Good behaviour should be praised.

- Make lists for the student to follow during the day.

- Students may need a list taped to their desk.

- Some students with special needs and/or developmental disabilities may have difficulty relating chalk board instructions to their own behaviour.

- Shelves and book cases should be enclosed if possible to eliminate visual distraction.

- Use vivid colours to emphasize important concepts.

- Emphasize with sound and movement the factors that complement the learning objectives.

- During organized activities, hyperactive students need structure.

- Students need sequence of activity.

- Students need to know what is expected of them.

- Students need to know what behaviours will be acceptable.

- Loosely structured activities must be balanced with highly structured activities to give the student opportunity to move about, visit, relax, etc.

- Provide structure and predictable routine.

- Limit time frames for one activity to no more than 30 minutes if possible.

- Limit type/number of new situations encountered at one time.

- Anticipate - know danger signs/situations.

- Teach substitute behaviours when they can't keep hands off others.

- Provide lessons which emphasize manual/physical expression.

- Don't keep child in from break-time as they need to have breaks from the classroom environment.

- Short breaks during the day.

- Protect from over-stimulation.

- Control the watching of TV

- Reduce/control complexity of assigned tasks.

- Teach child to self-monitor.

- Help child get back under control if necessary.

- Stress listening skills.

- Visualize activity level.

- Have a plan in place for "quiet time" when child feels overwhelmed.

- For long waits, give something to do with their hands (textured toy).

- Focus on specifics to increase attention during reading.

SOCIAL BEHAVIOUR

Enforcing good social behaviour is very important and must be started as soon as possible, as these are the values that will help throughout life. You want your child to be accepted and welcomed wherever you go. No one wants a disruptive child and then later an adult. What is cute at 18 months is NOT cute at 18 years! We are very proud that we can take Tisha anywhere, but we do explain to her where we are going and why so that she can prepare herself for the experience.

Poor social adaptation, lack of awareness of social behaviour and poor judgement lead to difficulty in establishing friendships and has the potential for social isolation or exploitation. While Fetal Alcohol Spectrum Disorder students may be outgoing and socially engaging, they can be perceived as overly talkative, intrusive, impulsive, hyperactive, and demand attention, even if the attention is negative. There is a discrepancy between their verbal skills and the ability to communicate effectively.

- Show the child how to share activities

- Teach the child how to be a friend.

- Use puppets or dolls to explain concepts.

- Teach the child how to sit with a friend at the table.

- Emphasize feelings of others.

- Practice using manners, consideration statements and apologies.

- Use peer tutoring as the FAS child will learn from others correct behaviours.

- Pair up children for a week so the child with special needs and/or developmental disabilities can learn from children who do not have special needs and/or developmental disabilities.

- Allow students with special needs and/or developmental disabilities to help other students.

- Capitalize on academic strengths of the student with special needs and/or developmental disabilities.

Treat students with special needs and/or developmental disabilities as valuable, worthwhile human beings with gifts to share. All students see teachers and other school personnel as role models and will follow the examples they set.

Teachers may need to work with the school counsellor in the following areas:

- Inappropriate sexual behaviour

- Depression

- Isolation

- Loneliness

- Inappropriate expectations for work, school, and independence

Be firm, and realistic about expectations and performance from students

TEACHING SOCIAL SKILLS.

Help the child be more aware of how people express their feelings non-verbally, i.e. model different facial expressions, hand on hip, arms akimbo, etc.

Teach:

- How to accept criticism or negative feedback

- How to show someone you like them

- Getting adult attention in a positive way

- How to ask for something

- How to greet another person

- How to start a conversation

- How to give and take a compliment

- How to handle anger

- How to say no to peer pressure

- How to act when riding public transport

- How to accept disappointment

- What to do when someone hurts their feelings

- What to do when they are feeling scared

- How to ignore someone who is bothering them

- How to disagree with someone in an appropriate way

SELF ESTEEM BUILDING:

> We encourage Tisha with all her strengths so as to give her confidence. She likes to tell people that she is special and has been on TV. It is so important for all concerned to build self esteem and self confidence and ensure the person with FAS is encouraged in the areas in which they do well. Do not make an issue over things that are not achievable. Everything is RE-PEAT, REPEAT, REPEAT until you sound like a broken record.

- Recognize successes each day

- Model alternative behaviours

- Rehearse social skills

- Test knowledge, not attention span

- Positive incentives for finishing a task

- Encourage

- Recognize partially correct responses

- Encourage use of positive self talking

- Give attention to children who are behaving appropriately

- If child is discouraged over repeating mistakes, stress they are just getting another chance

- Avoid asking 'Why' questions

- Have child write or talk about something that they know and have done

- Have child teach the class about something they know well

- Foster independence in self help, play/learning activities

- Treat child with respect & dignity

- Encourage use of positive self talk

- Encourage decision making

- Reward more than punish

- Encourage child lead adult/child play

- Help child see value of failure

- Encourage child to self monitor

- Work on child's body/self image

- Advocate the child to try first before asking for help

- Offer support, not criticism

- Focus on daily living/survival skills

- Encourage to help as valued member of family

- Put problem solving strategies list in conspicuous place. These could be- what to do in an emergency, who to phone for help

- Encourage child to use language to ask for what they want not to shout or cry

- Emphasize what the child can do and focus positively on progress made

AVOID USING THE SAME TIRED PHRASES AND REINFORCEMENTS.

Rather Try These Alternatives:

• Now you have it!	• That's sensational	• Dynamite work
• This makes my day	• Fabulous	• Your personal best
• Excellent	• Nobody does it better	• Now you have the hang of it
• You've mastered this	• You're learning quickly	• You really outdid yourself
• Exceptional	• Great job	• Great going
• Terrific	• You're unreal	• Outstanding
• That's it	• You make it look easy	• Awesome
• Keep up the good work	• Impressive	• Marvellous work
• This is too easy for you.	• You are very good at this	• That's the best ever
• Good work	• This was first class work	• That's just super
• Great effort today	• Good for you!	• Stupendous!

ANGER / STRESS MANAGEMENT

> I have never used medication or a special diet with Tisha, but this is not to say that these things could be necessary for other children. I am against Ritalin as this is a personality altering drug and I have been reliably informed by doctors that it does not help anyone with FAS.

- Fixation can be overcome through use of distractions (in subtle, calm manner)

- Aggression / hitting can be re-directed (use of quiet space, tactile display)

- Acknowledgement of feelings associated with behaviour displayed

- Create leadership opportunities through sport, music, re-alistic responsibilities

DISCIPLINE

With discipline, a well structured environment will help, with the same routines. If the routine has to be changed, do not just 'do it' but explain in advance why and what will happen instead. Going to a new place or situation can make the child upset and because of them not being able to express feelings, stress could result in tantrums. Tisha starts shaking and hangs on to us when confronted with what she considers unusual. We then either distract her or if that fails, leave. Sometimes we do not know what the problem is. She has a fear of Father Christmas, security guards, people in costumes and loud noises. The decorations and lights at Christmas are very difficult for her to handle.

- Be firm, but supportive

- Redirect behaviour

- Ignore negative behaviour when possible

- Do not debate

- Specifically label obnoxious behaviour

- Make "My choice" cards. These would be where a child could explain feelings or behaviour

- Guide to solutions

- Past behaviour is valuable guide

- Set limits and consistently follow them, eg a toy must be put away before another is taken out

- Limit time child expected to sit quietly

- Talk about cause and effect relationships

- Avoid threats

- Be brief.

- Reinforce school rules

- Change rewards often to keep interest high

- Use time out when behaviour is excessive

- Negative behaviour may be symptom of unmet needs

- Avoid getting involved in child's temper tantrums

- Tell children exactly what you want them to do.

- Review and repeat consequences of behaviour

- Anticipate danger signs/situations and plan ahead

- Avoid statements that place a value on behaviour

- Don't debate over rules/infractions. "Just do it."

- Notice when doing / behaving well / appropriately

- Work on compliance

- Model/encourage self-talk to help control impulsivity

- Don't expect child's fear to prevent them from doing something dangerous

- Focus on getting attention in ways other than negative behaviour or crying

- When all else fails – repeat, repeat

- Observe, Recognition, Modify

- Child may appear to understand more than he/she does

- Acknowledgement of DIFFERENCES in all children

- Importance of body language

Create Leadership

- Give a child a task to be responsible for a week

- E.g. Collecting work books

- Giving out work books

- Tidying up

- Give out sport equipment

- Put away toys

TANTRUMS

> We find that redirecting the beginnings of frustration, irritation and sensory problems work well. We pick up when something is beginning to bother Tisha by recognising her body language, then we will talk to her about another subject or simply leave and go somewhere else.

Let the student know there is a protocol for loss of control. Taking the student's hand and holding it a short time will give the student a signal that the teacher thinks the student is losing control. If the restraint is necessary (danger to self or others), the teacher needs to exercise care and control. Talk to the student, telling him/her that you are helping him/her to control his/her behaviour. "I am going to hold on to you until you are calm. Are you feeling better? Let me know when you are ready for me to let go."

Look for behaviours which may signify visual problems - abnormal head posturing, squinting, holding paper close to face, obvious errors made when working from the chalk board.

If the student has an extremely difficult time with loud noises and lots of activity, the student should be taught in a relatively quiet and calm area.

Remain calm and quiet

- Take the child to a different room. Lullaby music playing in the room may help calm the child

- Hold the child

- Caregiver/teacher's body language should not get the child excited. Talk in a calm voice, walk slowly. If the teacher is relaxed, this will help the child relax

Determine what happened before the tantrum occurred. Look for the start to the behaviour

- Previous circumstances are the events/things that happen which help the child lose his/her temper

- Look at different ways to eliminate the chances of the child throwing a tantrum

- Another way of reducing the likelihood of the child having a tantrum is to teach the child new ways of dealing with his/her stress. Teach the child to say "I'm cross".

- Child's diet could be contributing factor for the behaviour. Observe the child for any health problems

- An ear infection may cause the child to pull at his/her ears. Ask the child to "Show me where you hurt."

Ignore negative behaviour whenever possible

- Avoid over reacting to negative behaviour

- Build a positive reinforcement

- If the child does not need sleep at nap time, the child may benefit from having active activities - ride tricycle in the hall.

ATTENTION DEFICIT

Determine how long the child is working on an activity.

- If the child is drawing circles on a paper and the child decides to quit, have the child draw "one more" circle.

- The teacher should never make the child do the activity more than once if the teacher said "draw one more circle".

- This approach should increase the child's attention span over time.

- Once the teacher has determined the attention span for an activity, expand it by one more try and reinforce the student with praise.

- Determine what activity the student can attend to longest. What is it about that activity that allows him/her to attend? Generalize these features to other activities.

Tisha can concentrate for long periods of time when playing computer games – Tisha's favourite is Zoo Tycoon and the more difficult Zoo Tycoon II, both of which she plays for hours. She is able to recognise the symbols and words and through play is being educated.

INCREASING ATTENTION SPAN:

- Give anticipatory explanations

- Novelty is an excellent attention getter

- Use head phones to block out any outside distractions

- Present topic to create curiosity

- Control classroom interruptions

- Use cues to start and stop, such as clapping or a whistle

- Use eye contact, touch, call name

- Outline to increase comprehension

- Describe/compare objects, events, details

- Ask child to paraphrase directions given to them

- Vary loudness, inflection/quality of voice

- Slowly increase sustained attention

- Random participation

- Omit key words from rhymes, so that the child has to fill it in

- Focus attention with pictures/objects

- Child completes several items, then check to ensure they understand task

Tisha doing homework.
Tisha used to astonish us by doing jig saw
puzzles with the picture facing down.

CHAPTER 3
ACADEMIC DEVELOPMENT

Tisha tries very hard with reading and writing and when her school took her out of the reading programme, we enrolled her in an after school programme called Kumon. She goes twice a week and is making progress. She loves copying words. Tisha recognises lots of logos, public information signs and many words.

ACADEMIC DEVELOPMENT

Children with fetal alcohol spectrum disorder are usually learning disabled and the more damage from alcohol there is the more likely they are to exhibit multiple learning problems.

While such students may gain basic reading and writing skills, they often have poor comprehension and problem solving abilities. They exhibit short attention spans and memory problems. Skills seem to be acquired but even short term checking will indicate they have lost the skill or parts of it. They do not realise that there are consequences to their behaviour as they do not know right from wrong, therefore are easily led astray.

Respect of others' property should be enforced by repetition, role play, story telling (also let the negative action happen to them in this enforcement). With regression set realistic expectations since it reduces the self-esteem of the learner (overcome this by focussing on the positive, staying in the present, talk on the behaviour NOT the child)

COLLABORATION BETWEEN TEACHER AND CAREGIVER

It is essential for the caregiver to be able to talk with the teacher, this can be frustrating as many teachers think they know more than the caregivers, but often the caregiver knows how to handle certain situations better. Also children react differently at home. It is good to remind them that you are working together for the good of the child. It is not a question of telling the teachers their job but trying to help. A lot of difficult situations can be avoided and the learning process made easier. This is a two way street as the caregiver could also learn some management skills. We have dealt with many teachers and most of them were receptive to what we had to say and understood that it is not that Tisha won't but rather that she can't.

Collaboration is a must, and education for children with FASD requires a multifaceted approach. It can be difficult to convince professionals used to working independently to band together. However, no one discipline is able to do it all. "I" must give way to "we" so that an interdependent group is formed that includes caregivers and professionals. FASD children require a united effort to solve their problems and enhance their learning and lives.

There must be a free exchange of information. Teachers need to know what the caregivers and doctors know. If caregivers do not offer insights, then teachers must seek out the information. Good home/school communication is an absolute necessity.

A variety of specialists will be required to meet the needs of students with FASD. The main challenge with physical, occupational and speech specialists is convincing them that the child is truly different from the "normal" disabled child. Because these students often look normal and are so engaging, it is easy for a therapist to treat the child less aggressively than is necessary.

Classroom aides are often needed to assist with keeping the child on task. Aides can help the child work on academic, social, or behavioural goals.

Professionals who are called on to collaborate will likely have to do a lot of research on their own. Much can also be learned from the families of children with FAS. These are often the true experts. They have been, in many cases, living with FAS long before it was diagnosed, before any research studies were begun. They have learned a lot about what not to do and what works that can be passed along to professionals seeking their advice and knowledge.

Professionals should take advantage of in-service training. They also need to learn how to listen to understand, not reply. Professionals need to listen to learn about a particular child. While the child may fit many of the defined characteristics of FAS, it is likely that he or she will have almost as many individual characteristics. Being flexible, creative and open are important characteristics for all of those who work with FASD students.

Professionals should strive to give good information. If a professional doesn't really know, he or she can give advice that is totally out of step with the needs of the child. This is truly frustrating to caregivers who, acting upon that advice, see their child fail to progress or worse, see them regress.

EVALUATION AND ASSESSMENT OF THE CHILD

> Assessments by a developmental clinic are very necessary and we were so lucky to have the best, this will show where help is needed e.g. Occupational Therapy or Physiotherapy. Also it is a guide as to where the child will need to be schooled.

Testing usually includes a standardized IQ test and Child Behaviour Checklist. The test data should be used to develop a detailed needs statement. Caregivers and guardians must insist on yearly testing. What appears to be normal progress can become a major delay very quickly; and without repeated testing, the lack of progress will be missed.

The following evaluations may be helpful in learning more about the child's development and assist in planning the teacher's activities.

- Speech and language evaluations

- Psychological evaluations

- Motor evaluations

- Adaptive behaviour

Children with special needs and/or developmental disabilities usually need more one-to-one teaching. The number of staff available for the number of children with special needs and/or developmental disabilities needs to be a consideration.

The students with special needs and/or developmental disabilities usually need repetition of the information.

EARLY INTERVENTION

> Early intervention is vitally important. The exper-
> tise of the specialists we were lucky enough to see
> were able to guide and help when we needed it
> and we were able to help them in practical things.
> They were also able to assess what other special-
> ists Tisha needed to see. I was told that the early
> years are when the most learning is achieved as
> the learning skills diminish in the teenage years.

Diagnosis at birth and early intervention is the most critical part of treating children whose central nervous system has suffered damage from alcohol. Children who get early services are more likely to have a positive outcome.

Current brain research indicates that ages 0 to 2 are the most active growth period of the brain. Children must be stimulated through touch, speech and images to develop fully.

CURRICULUM

- Strict curricula have not been found to be effective for students with Fetal Alcohol Spectrum Disorders because they do not allow for individualization.

- Curriculum needs to be flexible to meet the child's needs.

- The students must proceed at their own speed based on developmental abilities.

- Trying to push the child into a specific grade or curricu-lum because of chronological age is a frustrating experi-ence for everyone.

- Mastery learning, where each objective in the curriculum is mastered before proceeding to the next objective, is more effective.

- These children need to over learn, to learn mastery while allowing for memory deficit.

- Social and behavioural proficiency must be incorporated into the curriculum specifically.

- Competence in communication must be stressed. Children with FASD tend to be "word wise", appearing to have more language ability than is actually theirs.

- Sometimes a child will use misbehaviour to communicate. A teacher must be able to recognize these attempts and then provide the language for the child so he or she can become more effective.

- Small children need to be taught how to communicate needs, interact with peers, and respond to others appropriately. Older children need to be taught give and take communication.

- Effective educational programmes target functional skills. Adaptations, money skills, meal preparation, job performance and use of transportation are just some of the everyday kinds of things they need to know.

- Training the child to be an effective adult has priority over Mathematics, however, academic subjects should be pursued as long as there is forward progress.

- Curricula should be outcome-based and should be a transition for the student to adult life. Creativity, flexibility, and beginning with the end in mind are helpful techniques when planning and delivering curricula for FASD children.

TEACHING METHODS

Our school experiences have been quite varied. Our most positive and beneficial to Tisha was when she attended the normal schools. The first playschool and the pre-primary she attended, the teachers were wonderful and Tisha was accepted and never made to feel different. Allowances were made if she couldn't do a task that the other children could do. She thrived at both these schools.

ELSEN SCHOOLS present Education for Learners with Special Educational Needs

She has attended three ELSEN schools and unfortunately has not made a lot of progress in the academic subjects. Tisha loves school as she is a very social person and enjoys the company of her peers. We feel a lot of opportunities have been lost for Tisha as the class teachers have so many disabilities and skill levels to cope with, even in a small class of 15 students.

Her skill level is that of a grade one learner for reading. She is able to count but has no understanding of numbers. When she goes shopping everything costs R5.00

Time is also a difficult concept for Tisha as things either happened yesterday or tomorrow.

This also applies to the hours in the day and morning and evening always have to be explained.

**Direct instruction has been shown to be
an effective instructional approach**

- The modelling, prompting and checking sequence of direct instruction allows the student to reach accuracy

- Speed is then built with repeated drill and practice until proficiency is reached

- Checks are used to ensure the skill is retained. Children with FASD need to over learn skills

- Sign Language has been shown to help non-deaf children learn communication and language skills

- Some FASD children have responded positively when sign language and an oral language are used together. Sign Language is a concept language and using it adds both the visual and tactile senses. Sign provides the structure, the concrete picture, a child needs for clarity and content. It uses a different part of the brain from language. Because it is tactile rather than spoken, it forces the child to slow down and think, thereby improving sequencing.

- A bi-modal and bi-lingual approach can be effective where a single channel for communication and learning may not be sufficient to help the child.

- Computer Assisted Learning can be used to teach and practice skills that need to be over learned. Computers are patient and can provide the thousands of trials necessary for learning to take place. An hour spent practising just two plus two does not irritate a computer, but could discourage a human teacher.

- Hands-on learning is preferred

- Programmes should be community-based and have generalization as the outcome. Opportunities for practice outside the classroom need to be structured.

- Find the child's strengths and use them to the advantage. For example, a child who has a strength in music may use rhythms and rhymes to help him remember such things as addresses and phone numbers.

- Make learning fun, but set and enforce limits consistently and firmly.

- The teacher needs to see the alcohol-impaired child as an individual who faces challenges rather than a broken child and work to help the child develop good self-esteem.

CLASSROOM STRUCTURE

Structure is absolutely critical.
Left to their own devices,
FASD children follow impulsive tendencies.

- Teachers need to establish a routine and keep it faithfully. A set routine can help meet the life-skill needs of FASD students.

- Transitions are difficult for FASD children. The child needs to be alerted ahead of time and then guided through the transition. It may be necessary to assign a peer to help the student stay on task during class changes or during other unsupervised times.

- Class size needs to be kept to a minimum. FASD students need individual attention. The teacher needs to have time for one on one activities.

- There should be a classroom aide

- The room should be bright and cheerful without a multitude of distractions

- One thing at a time is better

- Cover over bulletin boards until they are needed

- Because of compulsive or impulsive behaviours, the child may have problems settling down if overly stimulated by the classroom environment

- If there is something new in the room, allow the child to thoroughly explore it. Supervise the activity and use it to develop language.

- Rules are enforced in a consistent way

- Establish a few simple rules

- Give the student reminders for ending and beginning of activities. Use tactual signal- touch shoulder, tap elbow

- Consistent routine.

- Provide diaries. Class periods should not exceed 20 minutes

- Students with special needs and/or developmental disabilities need several breaks during the day

- Students may need sleep during the day

- Students may need to get up and move around more frequently than other students

- Plan activities to facilitate movement and creativity between work assignments

- Students with special needs and/or developmental disabilities may need food snacks during the day

Managing classroom distractions:

- Try putting up only the work of the week

- Do not clutter the walls with posters – weather charts, etc.

- Bring out each item as it is needed

- Try learning one colour at a time, for instance have a yellow day, clothes, food, painting etc.

Application to physical class structure:

- Distracters are walls, windows, fluorescent lights

- Beneficial is low tone / soft music

- Create a quiet area

CLASSROOM CONDITIONS

Application to learners:

- Have a fun item / exercise before lessons (action songs)

- Maintain eye contact through directed speech (body language is difficult to read)

- REPETITION (facilitates learning since there may be a problem with short term memory)

- Time out discipline methods (taking away body contact since facial expressions are not recognized). Must be short/simple/immediate/calm

- Some children are tactile defensive (therefore create more opportunities for stimulation)

- Having the right tools, such as calculator, head phones, computer etc.

TRANSITIONAL PERIODS:

- Egg timer clearly defines end of a task

- Use visual time cues

- Songs or music/rhythm cues can be used, or a

- Verbal early warning system

PHYSICAL ENVIRONMENT

- It will be necessary to dim the lights for nap time.

- No fluorescent lights

- Soft calm music may relax the environment during breaks

- May be able to use headphones for quiet time and concentration

- Students with special needs and/or developmental disabilities are not always able to block out other noises

- The ticking of the clock can distract the students with special needs and/or developmental disabilities

- Teacher talking with another student can distract students with special needs and/or developmental disabilities

- The environment should be structured and predictable.

- Well defined areas

- Preferential seating

- Use same staff consistently

- Get child involved

- The child must sit with feet flat on the floor or on a book to feel 'grounded'

- When over stimulated get child to put head on desk

Tisha, 16 years old

CHAPTER 4
EDUCATIONAL
RECOMMENDATIONS

> Tisha had problems with speech and so had speech therapy. At first we used a sign language which Tisha developed to let us know what she wanted. If we could not understand she would throw herself backwards in frustration. How she never cracked her skull I will never know! As soon as she could talk this ceased. To this day she has to make an effort to swallow as her lip is low toned, so when excited, she tends to dribble.

LANGUAGE DEVELOPMENT

Students with special needs and/or developmental disabilities may have delayed language development

- Begin with simple story books

- The teacher can touch an object and name the object for the child

- Use real objects like "trees, cars, dog" and name the object

- If the child says "drink" say to the child "more drink" to stimulate more words in the child's vocabulary. Expand the child's vocabulary slowly - when the child starts using two words, start using three words "want more drink".

- Talk with the child at the child's level - use short sentences - avoid using long sentences

- A speech therapist would be a good resource for child and teacher

- The teacher needs to use proper pronunciation

- Always use the child's name at the start of all sentences

- Meal time - have the child say what he/she wants rather than just give the child what one thinks the child wants

- Music activities can help children learn vocabulary as they seem to learn using rhythm

- Use basic language when giving instructions

- Avoid giving more than one instruction per sentence

- Make sure he/she understands directions given

- Articulation errors are common - accept their communications without correcting them. Repeat the sounds correctly

- Quality verses quantity of speech

- Listen for the number of words per sentence

- Listen for the number of new words that the student uses

- Reinforce concept development through concrete examples encouraging the child to demonstrate understanding. Example –weather and temperature - child would know what to wear on a hot day and what to wear on a cold day.

MATHS DEVELOPMENT

- Memorized counting from one to ten does not mean the child understands the numbers.

- Teach the child to learn what the number "one" means before any more numbers are taught to the child, for example say "Give me one crayon"; "Put one toy on the table".

- Cut the numbers out of paper - glue oatmeal, rice, glitter, etc. to the number - the child can see, feel, and hear the number.

- Touch and count objects.

- Teach functional math - money, time, addition, subtraction.

- Using the students' fingers for addition and subtraction or a calculator may assist in teaching students with special needs and/or developmental disabilities. These techniques should not be the first choice but should not be ruled out if they can benefit the student's ability to learn maths. A calculator may be necessary for the student to do multiplication and division.

- Maths seems to be the more difficult subject for the students with special needs and/or developmental disabilities.

- Memorizing the multiplication table may not be successful with all students who have special needs and/or developmental disabilities. Division may also be a difficult concept.

- Spend extra time on decimal points in math,(spelling, etc.) because of inattention to detail

- Provide practice of maths facts with a computer that gives immediate feedback

- Find opportunities for child to apply maths to real life

- Put maths problems with same process on single line or sheet

- Make operation symbols extra large, bold, or colour coded

SENSORY STIMULATION

> Tisha loves to feel things and will play for ages with squishy, gooey things. There are a few things that annoy her such as labels in clothing; some children with FAS cannot even stand the seams, so wear their clothes inside out.

USE AS MUCH SENSORY STIMULATION
AS POSSIBLE TO TEACH EACH CONCEPT

Example - teaching the colour "blue"

- Wear blue clothes

- Paint with blue paint

- Use blue construction paper for projects

USE OBJECTS AS MUCH AS POSSIBLE TO TEACH CONCEPTS

Example - teaching the children about "circles"

- Laminate polka dot fabric

- Use a pastry cutter to cut circle sandwiches

- Cut circles from construction paper

TEACHING ACTIVITIES MUST BE "CONCRETE"

- Give child choices he/she can see, feel, touch and hear

- Provide hands on materials whenever possible

- Take students to actual places to teach learning objectives

- Allow students to make concrete choices. Example - "Which one do you want?

HAND EYE COORDINATION ACTIVITIES

The teacher may need to show the child the object, show the child how to do the activity, guide the child through the activity, and then encourage the child to do the activity on his/her own.

- The teacher could pick up the puzzle piece for the child to put in the right place in the puzzle.

- Use puzzles with knobs on the pieces.

- The teacher may need to make a larger lace card from cardboard. The lace for the lace card may need masking tape on the end to make it easier for child to lace the card. The teacher could lace the first two holes of a lacing card.

- Putting pegs in a board

- Pounding a peg board

- Picking up things with tweezers

- Tapestry

Let student help with tasks that require sorting, stapling, putting things in place, etc.

ORGANIZATIONAL SKILLS:

> We have tried in vain to teach Tisha to be organised but she just can't manage this. She never remembers where she puts things and then the hunt is on! We may find one shoe in one room and the other shoe in another!

- Check lists with photos, pictures and words

- Putting on deodorant

- Cleaning teeth

- Where different clothes should go

- READING AND WRITING SKILLS

- ALPHABET

- Make letters with paper and glue other objects to the letter

- Match letters

- Match words

- Use the sounds of the letters repeatedly – J   juice, jump, jacket, etc.

- Teacher cuts a letter out of sandpaper and has the child follow the sandpaper letter with his/her finger

- Teacher writes a letter on the blackboard and has the child trace the letter on the blackboard

- Teacher makes dots on a paper in the shape of a letter and has the child connect the dots to make the letter, gradually decreasing the number of dots to connect to make the letter

- When a child is learning to write his/her name, it may be easier for the child if the child uses all capital letters at the beginning

- Match letters to objects. "A - Apple".

- Match letters to pictures

- Follow the above sequence with words

- Generalize new words into other activities, other class work and home activities

- Have a "Letter for the Day"

- Use green and red clues to indicate the beginning and ending of a word to facilitate proper writing of letters

READING

Some students may have difficulty focusing their eyes on the left side of the page and moving their eyes to the right.

If student uses a piece of paper to follow the line across the page, the student may have an easier time reading.

Use green marker at the left side changing to red at the right side for written work

Used coloured arrows to signal starting points and direction from left to right

Use books with simple, plain, pictures. Small detailing marks in a picture can distract the student

Provide the student with books that follow student's interest and independent reading levels

Independent reading levels means the student can read 90% of the words in the book

Read aloud to the students daily and provide uninterrupted silent reading periods

Encourage reading for enjoyment and developing independence

Incorporate popular magazines, newspapers, school paper, into reading programme

Emphasize reading as a means to communication. Note writing, letter writing, memos, posters, etc.

Rewrite directions at a lower reading level

Highlight key words

Use large print/talking books

Use cognitive mapping

Make a picture dictionary

Use materials with simple illustrations

Tape record stories so can listen and read along

Avoid phonics to teach reading, as the child will have to re-learn at a later stage unless processing skills are adequate

Turning on Christmas lights in Adderley Street

Tisha in front, 5 years old

CHAPTER 5
LIVING WITH A CHILD
WITH FAS

Tisha was such a loving little girl that the rest of the family fell in love with her even though there were problems. Everybody helped with her and still do. As Tisha came to us as a new born, all difficulties were taken in their stride. I suppose because we had babies with other problems, my children were very good with her and the other babies who joined our family. I couldn't have wished for better children with the capacity to love and accept new members to the family.

PHYSICAL DEVELOPMENT

Physical development is very slow and weight gain very little. When Tisha was a baby, visits to the clinic were a bit embarrassing as Tisha was so slow to put on any weight.

I was advised that the milestones would be severely delayed, but Tisha's were not too bad because of all the physiotherapy she had. We had such a wonderful Physiotherapist, who helped and taught me so much.

Puberty is a new area for us now that Tisha is becoming a young lady and we have new problems to overcome. We have had to put Tisha on to the birth control injection as she could not possibly cope with her periods, from both a hygiene point of view and emotionally.

Tisha took part in a DVD made at her school, which explained a lot of things for her in a very sensitive and practical way. Also, it reinforced the idea that it is alright to say 'NO' if you should feel uncomfortable or don't want to be touched. This has to be constantly explained to her by us.

WHAT CAN CAREGIVERS DO ON BEHALF OF THEIR CHILD?

For all mothers, I think, it is easier to do things for the child, such as pulling a jersey over the head. It is so important to let the child try and try again but be careful to watch for signs of frustration and stop. Start again later or the next day. The frustration for the mother and teacher is the child forgetting what you were sure had been mastered. I still have to check whether Tisha has put on deodorant and brushed her teeth. This can be especially trying for a teacher as the 'reading done yesterday is forgotten the next day. When this happens, I call it Tisha unplugged. The funny thing is that some things are retained and resurface months or years later.

- Thank teachers for help/efforts/understanding

- Emphasize your awareness of how hard their job is

- Ask teachers how you can help

- Write occasional personal notes to your child's teacher to maintain communication and to ask about progress or follow up comments or concerns

- Let your child see you and the teacher working together on his/her behalf

- Attend classroom or school events

- Comment on or recognize the teacher's strengths, when you can

- Start a FASD support group for caregivers of children with FASD

- Start a FASD support group for people with FASD

- Provide respite care for a family with FASD children

- Lobby for in-services on FASD at your school, for all staff, community members and caregivers

- Tell your paediatrician about FASD and take informational materials to them about FASD

- Recommend to Government that they learn about FASD implications

- Attend conferences on FASD

- Be an advocate for addicted mothers

- Encourage your college and medical schools to run courses on Alcohol Related Birth Defects

- Lobby for social workers and caregivers to be required to have training in ARBD

- Share information/material that you have with others working with these children

- Get caregivers with FASD children to the PTA (school's Parent Teacher Association) so their interests are represented

PROVIDING STRUCTURE FOR HOME ROUTINES:

- Get everything ready for school before going to bed

- Establish a few simple rules.

- Use same language repetitively

- Develop Hello and Farewell rituals

> Our hello and farewell rituals are fairly simple really, a kiss and a hug goodbye and "How did you get on, what did you do?" when she is greeted after going out.

- Establish routines so future events can be predicted

- Explain when visiting a new place

- Encourage child to finish activity before starting the next one

- Give auditory and visual advance warning that the activity will soon be over

- Clearly define child's space. Young children especially need a "place".

REINFORCERS AND ACTIVITIES FOR CAREGIVERS TO TRY:

- Go to the library and get some books

- Write a letter to a friend or relative with your child

- Have your child draw a picture of the way he/she feels right now

- Fly a kite

- Go for a walk

- Make a greeting card

- Plant seeds for a small flower, herb, or vegetable garden of their own

- Write a story your child tells you

- Listen to a CD together

- Go outside after dark and star gaze together. Point out planets, familiar star formations

- Make a Wish

- Run through the sprinkler

- Make gift wrapping paper by decorating with stamps, stickers, sequins, feathers, or bright colours

- Make up a rhyme together

- Play I Spy

- Play card games

- Go down to a pond and gather some tadpoles. Watch them grow

- Play tossing the beanbag. Use a wastepaper basket or deep bowl to catch them in

- Do some baking

- Pick strawberries to make jam

- Do basket work

- Make holiday decorations

- Pick some flowers

- Watch a DVD or go to the movies

- Do some bead work

- Make play dough

- Play a "What if" game with your child. What if... there were no rules or laws? If there were no cars or streets?..................there were no houses?

- Ask who, what, when, why, and where as well as how - about topics

- Music games – action songs

- Basic exercise – star jumps

- Running on the spot

- Bending

- Stretching

VOCATIONAL EDUCATION

We feel that is never too early to start vocational education. We think it is far too late to start in the last year of school. The young should be well informed as to what a work place is like and what is expected of them. Be realistic but positive.

Continue practicing the basic skills necessary to live independently as adults.

Basic skills should be generalized to a variety of settings

- Use a variety of stimuli to elicit behaviour

- Use a variety of settings

- Use a variety of personnel

> Tisha will be able to work in a sheltered environment when the time comes and we will then explore what kind of work will best suit her skills.

Curriculum should focus on:

- Recognizing and coping with being labelled as "different."

- Assisting students to function as social human beings

- Understanding rules of social interaction

- Taking on responsibilities.

- Making decisions and realizing their consequences

- Developing and practicing independent living skills within a group setting - getting along with others in the same living space, sharing responsibilities, cooking, personal hygiene, etc.

- Assisting students to function in the world of work

- Identify individual interests and aptitudes

- Develop self scheduling skills, community mobility skills, rule governed behaviour, etc.

- Develop and practice job related skills

THIS IS THE FIRST LEAFLET VIVIEN
WROTE TO HELP OTHER CAREGIVERS

In 1996 there was no information available on
how to care for a baby with FAS
so I put this leaflet together,
as I was being contacted by care givers,
social workers, doctors and nurses for help.

Suggestions on Care of a
Fetal Alcohol Syndrome Baby

About Fetal Alcohol Syndrome

Fetal Alcohol Syndrome (FAS) is a birth defect caused by the mother drinking alcohol during pregnancy. It is diagnosed when the babies have:

Growth deficiency before and after birth for height or weight or both.

Characteristic facial features are generally short eye slits, a flat mid face, a short upturned nose. The ridges between the nose and lips are smooth or long and a thin upper lip.

Some central nervous system damage including a small size of brain, tremors, hyperactivity, fine or gross motor problems

Fetal Alcohol Syndrome is
100% Preventable
and 100% Irreversible.

About Me

I am a foster mother of a little girl who has Fetal Alcohol Syndrome (FAS). When I got her, she was 10 weeks old and I was told that her future did not look very good. However, with a great deal of love and help she has amazed everyone. I have also been foster mother to other FAS babies and have written this leaflet in the hope it will help other mothers to overcome some of the problems I have come across.

Basic Care

Fetal Alcohol Syndrome babies have many problems.

Understand that your baby's brain works differently.

Your baby could be very sensitive to touch, so before holding your baby wrap him/her snugly in a soft blanket.

Hold your baby for all feeds

Use soft lighting

Avoid loud noises, play soft calming music

Introduce new things like toys slowly and only when baby is calm and ready.

He/She may take longer in being able to sit up, crawl, walk, talk etc.

Sucking seems to be difficult and can be aided by laying baby in your lap and holding the cheeks to keep the lips around the teat. A feeding cup or spoon can be used, but it is important to get baby to suck. Honey on the dummy will encourage sucking and also helps to calm your baby.

Jerking

Jerking of the limbs when withdrawing from Alcohol can be eased by stroking and by wrapping tightly. At times some Fetal Alcohol Syndrome babies don't like to be touched, as it seems as if their nerve endings are raw. It has been found that there is usually one place that baby likes to be touched. One baby could be soothed by placing mother's mouth just below baby's ear and on another baby it was rubbing or patting the chest. Some gripe water has a lot of Alcohol in it and should be used sparingly but it can help a FAS baby when withdrawing from Alcohol. Holding baby with his/her back against your side and hanging over your arm also soothes. Alternatively, giving baby a warm bath may also help.

Dehydration

Babies that don't feed well, will also dehydrate very quickly so make sure baby gets plenty of fluids and if you are at all worried get baby to Doctor as quickly as possible.

Recipe for Rehydration fluid.

1 litre of boiled water and add 8 level teaspoons of sugar and 1/2 teaspoon of salt. Shake well and let baby drink as much as possible every 2 hours and after every dirty nappy.

Blocked Nose

To keep them clear, add 1/4-teaspoon salt or bicarbonate of soda to 1 cup of cooled boiled water and put one drop of this mixture in each nostril.

If baby has a lot of phlegm which makes feeding difficult, use a good pinch of Bicarbonate of Soda in a small drop of milk before feeding. This will help to bring the phlegm up.

Vomiting

If baby brings up a lot of milk after all feeds; Gaviscon® in the bottle may help or else in more severe cases Prepulsid®. This should be discussed with a doctor. Raising baby's head when lying in his/her cot seems to help - place a folded towel, blanket etc. under the mattress. When baby comes to eat solids he/she may not have the reflex to swallow so put in a mouthful of food, followed by the dummy.

General

If baby keeps his/her thumb tucked inside the fingers, at every opportunity place baby's thumb out flat and hold it in the open hand position on a flat surface.

If baby is constipated put a teaspoon of brown sugar in a drop of warm boiled water.

For upset stomach and fever try using;

One packet of Jelly dissolved in a cup of boiling water, stir in one and a half cups of cold water and leave to cool at room temperature (not in the fridge) and use as a drink.

CHAPTER 6
USEFUL CONTACT DETAILS

<u>SOUTH AFRICA</u>

- fasinfocentre@mweb.co.za

- www.fasdsa.org

- www.pebblesproject.co.za

- www.farr-sa.co.za

- www.earlyyearsservices.co.za

<u>INTERNATIONAL WEBSITES</u>

- www.come-over.to

- www.faslink.org

- www.betterendings.org

- www.acbr.com

- www.nofas-uk.org

- www.fasworld.com

- www.mcfares.org

- www.fasd-cmc.alberta.ca

- www.childstudy.org

- www.fan.org.nz

- www.ahw.org.nz

Thank you to everyone who has encouraged and supported me along the way

First and foremost my family Peter, Andrew, Melinda, David, Carrie, Leigh-Anne and Tisha

FASD Task Team – Sophia Warner, Sandra Marais, Anna-Susan Marais, Letitia Bosch, Maureen Mccrea, Rhenolda Davies, Avril Cupido, Estee Heyns, Andrea Engelbrecht, Peter and Vivien Lourens

FARR – Prof Denis Viljoen, Leana Olivier, Yumna Martin

Ann Myers – Physiotherapy

All the therapists

Clinic Sisters especially Sister Wright and Sister Pillay

Red Cross Childrens Hospital

Nurses and Receptionists at Red Cross Childrens Hospital

Prof Colleen Adnams

Dr. Steve Delport

Doctors in the many clinics

Shaheema Solomons

All members on FASlink

Peggy Oba

Ronnie Jurgens

Khulukazi Zimba

Vikki Osborn

Living with Fetal Alcohol Syndrome

Cape Town Child welfare

Jodee Kulp

Donovan Baguley

Joan Wright and her Kumon team

Friends and neighbours

Pinelands North Primary School (Red School)

Meerendal Pre-Primary School

Pinelands High School

Bel Porto School

Molenbeek School

Nancy Richards

The Media TV, radio and journalists

The group of friends who gave their support in starting International FAS Day

All the people who sent me material from overseas

FOR MORE INFORMATION PLEASE FEEL FREE TO CONTACT

fasinfocentre@mweb.co.za

0825099530

Made in the USA
Lexington, KY
06 April 2016